GETTING TO KNOW
THE U.S. PRESIDENTS

HERBERT
HOOVER

THIRTY-FIRST PRESIDENT
1929 – 1933

WRITTEN AND ILLUSTRATED BY MIKE VENEZIA

CHILDREN'S PRESS®
A DIVISION OF SCHOLASTIC INC.
NEW YORK   TORONTO   LONDON   AUCKLAND   SYDNEY
MEXICO CITY   NEW DELHI   HONG KONG
DANBURY, CONNECTICUT

Reading Consultant: Nanci R. Vargus, Ed.D., Assistant Professor, School of Education, University of Indianapolis

Historical Consultant: Marc J. Selverstone, Ph.D., Assistant Professor, Miller Center of Public Affairs, University of Virginia

Photographs © 2007: Alamy Images/Patrick Eden: 29; Corbis Images: 7, 31, 32 (Bettmann), 25 (Swim Ink 2, LLC), 17; Des Moines Art Center: 11 (Permanent Collections; Purchased jointly by the Des Moines Art Center and The Minneapolis Institute of Arts; with funds from the Edmundson Art Foundation Inc., Mrs. Howard H. Frank and the John R. Van Derlip Fund, 1982.2); Getty Images/Stock Montage: 3; Herbert Hoover Presidential Library: 13, 16, 18, 21, 24; Library of Congress: 30 (Dorothea Lange); Mary Evans Picture Library: 23; The Art Archive/Picture Desk: 6 (National Archives Washington DC); The Oakland Museum of California, City of Oakand, © the Dorothea Lange Collection, Gift of Paul S. Taylor: 8, 9.

Colorist for cover illustrations: Dave Ludwig
Colorist for interior illustrations: Andrew Day

Library of Congress Cataloging-in-Publication Data

Venezia, Mike.
    Herbert Hoover / written and illustrated by Mike Venezia.
        p. cm. — (Getting to know the U.S. presidents)
    ISBN-10: 0-516-22635-5 (lib. bdg.)   0-516-25211-9 (pbk.)
    ISBN-13: 978-0-516-22635-4 (lib. bdg.)   978-0-516-25211-7 (pbk.)
    1. Hoover, Herbert, 1874-1964—Juvenile literature. 2. Presidents—United States—Biography—Juvenile literature. I. Title.
    E802.V46 2007
    973.91'6092-dc22

                                                    2006000458

1 2 3 4 5 6 7 8 9 10 R 16 15 14 13 12 11 10 09 08 07

Herbert Hoover, the thirty-first president of the United States, was born in West Branch, Iowa, in 1874. When Herbert Hoover ran for president in 1928, he was just about the most popular person in the whole country. Only four years later, people had changed their minds. President Hoover had become one of the most disliked men in the United States.

The reason Herbert Hoover became so unpopular was that he was blamed for the country's problems during the Great Depression. The Great Depression was one of the worst periods in the history of the United States. It was a time when many people lost their jobs, cars, savings, and even their homes almost overnight!

The Great Depression started in 1929, only eight months after Herbert Hoover became president. It had actually been brewing for a long time. Then one big event really sent things downhill. On October 29, 1929, the New York Stock Market failed, or "crashed." A stock market is where shares in companies are traded. People had put a lot of money into the stock market and suddenly their investments were worthless.

This photograph by Dorothea Lange shows a family living in a trailer in Arizona during the Great Depression.

There were many reasons for the Great Depression. Most of them happened long before Herbert Hoover became president. For one thing, company and factory owners refused to give their workers raises. This kept the owners wealthy for a long time. Meanwhile, everyday workers had to borrow money from banks in order to buy cars, houses, furniture, radios, and even clothes.

Because of their low wages, workers found it almost impossible to pay back the banks. Sometimes they had to sell their property to raise money. Because they had very little money, people stopped buying goods. Then, since factories and stores weren't able to sell their products, they had to let their workers go, or even close down.

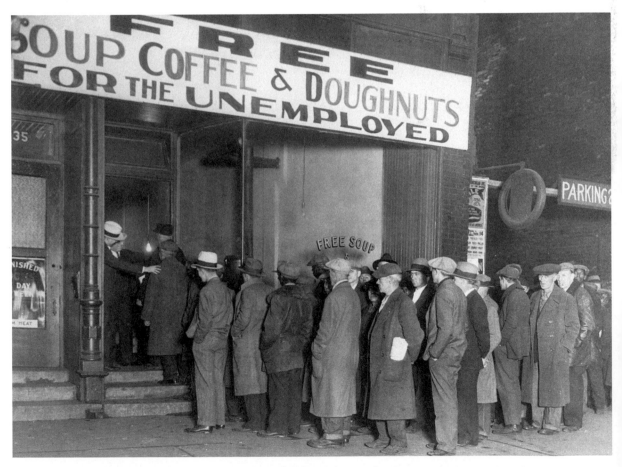

Unemployed men waiting in line at a soup kitchen during the Depression

Tractored Out, by Dorothea Lange

In the early 1920s, many people also made unwise and foolish investments and eventually lost all their money in the stock market. Farmers had grown too many crops, and could sell their corn and grain only at very low prices. Soon, many farmers lost their land and homes, too. Things kept getting worse and worse. The most serious part of the Depression, though, was that people were losing hope.

Man Beside Wheelbarrow, by Dorothea Lange

Herbert Hoover was born in the early 1870s, long before the Great Depression. His father was a blacksmith and his mother was a teacher. The Hoovers were also Quakers. The Quakers are a religious group that is totally against war. They believe strongly in world peace. Other Quaker values are the importance of education, simple living, honesty, and helping others.

The Birthplace of Herbert Hoover, by Grant Wood (Des Moines Art Center)

Quakers also feel that people can solve almost any problem if they cooperate and work together. These were beliefs that Herbert Hoover practiced throughout his life.

Sadly, by the time Herbert was nine years old, he had lost both of his parents. Mr. Hoover died of a heart attack when Herbert was only six years old. Then, just three years later, Mrs. Hoover passed away. Herbert and his brother and sister were suddenly orphans. The three Hoover children were passed around to live with different relatives while they grew up.

Herbert Hoover (right) at the age of fourteen with his brother Tad and sister Mary

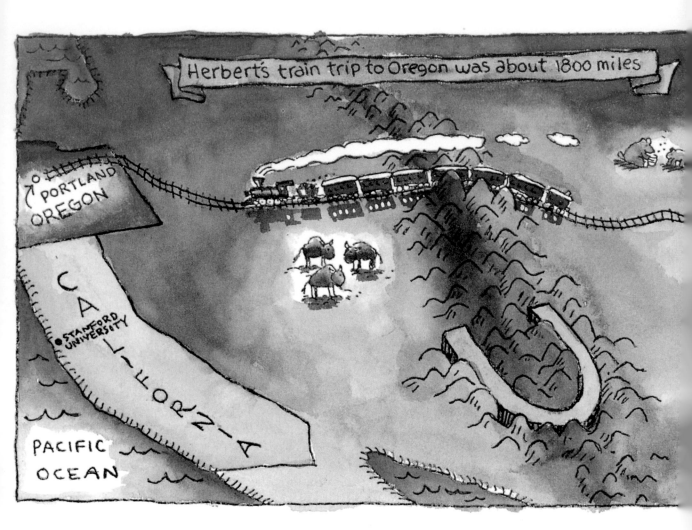

When Herbert was ten years old, his aunt and uncle asked him to come and live with them. A frightened and sad Herbert traveled hundreds of miles by train to the northwestern state of Oregon. Herbert's uncle was a doctor there. He also ran a school that Herbert attended as a teenager.

Living near the beautiful mountains and forests of Oregon gave Herbert a great appreciation for the outdoors. His favorite pastime was fishing in the crystal clear streams near his new home. When it was time to go to college, Herbert attended Stanford University in the nearby state of California.

Arthur Diggles
Herbert Hoover
R E McDonnell
James White
SURVEYING SQUAD - STANFORD UNIVERSITY IN 1893

To my good friend
Earnest Boyce from
R.E McDonnell

This photograph shows Herbert Hoover's surveying class at Stanford.
Hoover is seated on the left.

Herbert had decided to study geology. Geology is the study of what the earth is made of and how it was formed. Herbert hoped to become a mining engineer some day. During summer breaks, Herbert assisted geologists in different parts of the country.

Lou Henry on a porch rail at a sorority house at Stanford University

Herbert worked hard surveying the land and gathering rocks and mineral samples. During his time at Stanford, Herbert fell in love with the only female geology major at Stanford. Her name was Lou Henry. Lou loved the outdoors as much as Herbert did. Lou wasn't afraid to camp out in rugged areas or dig around for mineral samples all day in the hot sun. Lou loved fishing, too.

Herbert Hoover at a mining camp in Australia in 1900

Herbert and Lou both wanted to get married, but agreed to wait until Lou finished school and Herbert had a steady job. When Herbert graduated college, he didn't waste a moment. He took a job as a miner. For six months, Herbert worked harder than ever deep inside a California gold mine. Next, he got a job in the office of a mining expert. There, Herbert learned everything he needed to know about the mining business.

When Herbert was only twenty-three, a mining company asked him to head up their operations in Australia. Herbert's job was to find areas where there might be gold and silver and help improve existing mines. Herbert surprised people by solving almost any problem that popped up.

Because Herbert did such a great job in Australia, he was sent to China to manage mines there. Now Herbert was making enough money to support a wife. Before he traveled to China, Herbert stopped in California to marry Lou.

This photograph shows Lou Hoover inspecting a cannon at a Chinese fort.
The Hoovers were in China during the Boxer Rebellion of 1900.

In 1899, Herbert and Lou headed off to China. Shortly after they arrived, Herbert and Lou found themselves in the middle of a violent rebellion. A group of angry Chinese citizens wanted to get all foreigners out of their country. For almost a month, Herbert and Lou helped defend the town they lived in, until help arrived from the U.S. Army.

Herbert continued his successes in China and in many other countries as well. In 1908, Herbert decided to start his own mining business. Herbert, Lou, and their two sons traveled around, supervising mining operations and checking out new deals in Burma, Russia, Ethiopia, Egypt, South Africa, and Australia.

By the time Herbert Jr. was five, he had been around the world five times. Now Herbert Hoover wasn't just rich. He was super rich!

In 1914, world events changed Herbert's life forever. A war was beginning in Europe. The people of Belgium had become cut off from their food supply. Herbert Hoover was asked to head up an emergency rescue committee to save Belgium.

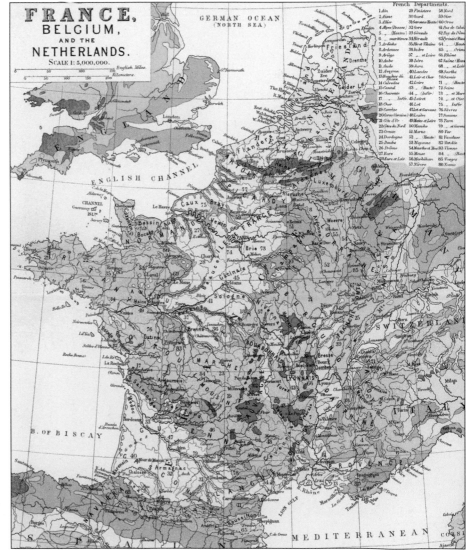

A map from the early 1900s showing France, Belgium, and the Netherlands

Hoover's Committee for the Relief of Belgium helped provide food for Belgian schoolchildren during World War I.

Herbert agreed to take on the job. He left his successful business and worked without pay. Herbert raised millions of dollars for food and medicine. He found ways to ship tons of food and deliver it directly to the people of Belgium.

In 1917 the United States entered World War I. President Woodrow Wilson asked Herbert to run an organization that conserved food and other needed supplies in the United States.

Herbert was so successful he became a household name. To "Hooverize" meant to voluntarily save food and not waste anything.

FOOD WILL WIN THE WAR
You came here seeking Freedom
You must now help to preserve it
WHEAT is needed for the allies
Waste nothing

UNITED STATES FOOD ADMINISTRATION

During World War I, Herbert Hoover ran the U.S. Food Administration. It produced posters like this one, which asked Americans to conserve food needed for the war.

Herbert Hoover became one of the most respected and well-known men in the country. After World War I ended, Herbert served as a close advisor to both President Harding and President Coolidge. As secretary of commerce, Hoover accomplished many important things. For example, he made sure many products and building materials were made in standard sizes. Before this time, factories could make plumbing and electrical supplies, car parts, nuts and bolts, and tools any way or size they wanted. Herbert's idea of standardizing saved people money and made their lives easier.

In 1927, when there was a terrible flood
on the Mississippi River, Herbert used his
skills to save people again. He quickly
supplied food and shelter to thousands of
flood victims all the way from Illinois to
the Gulf of Mexico.

In 1928, President Coolidge surprised people by deciding not to run for a second term. Members of the Republican Party immediately asked the popular Herbert Hoover to be their candidate for president. Herbert agreed, and easily beat the Democratic candidate, Al Smith.

President Hoover started out great in his new job. Right away he improved conditions for American Indians living on government reservations. He then added nearly two million acres to national forest preserves. President Hoover had construction started on a giant Colorado River dam.

Hoover Dam on the Colorado River at the Arizona-Nevada border

To this day, the Hoover Dam supplies water and electricity to millions of people in the southwestern states.

Migrant Mother,
by Dorothea Lange

When the Great Depression started, however, things began to go badly for President Hoover. He didn't seem to understand how serious the Depression really was. Even though people were asking the government for help, President Hoover didn't think it was a good idea simply to give people aid. He was afraid that giving people food and shelter or money might take away their desire to find jobs and work out problems for themselves.

But as the Depression got worse, most people were in way too much trouble to help themselves. Soon Herbert Hoover's name took on some new meanings. The shacks poor people were forced to live in were called "Hoovervilles." Empty pants pockets turned inside out were called "Hoover flags."

"Hooverville" on the outskirts of Seattle, Washington, in the early 1930s

Herbert Hoover ran for reelection in 1932, but he didn't have a chance of winning. Even though the Great Depression wasn't his fault, people blamed him for their problems. Herbert wasn't able to give the kind of help or leadership the American people needed.

Herbert Hoover lived to be ninety years old. He continued doing good works, helping supply needy countries with food and support. Unfortunately, the man who cared so much about people's welfare was often blamed for causing the Great Depression.

9288